THE RIGHT TO ABORTION:

A Psychiatric View

Also by the Group for the Advancement of Psychiatry
Normal Adolescence: Its Dynamics and Impact
(Formulated by the Committee on Adolescence)

THE RIGHT
TO ABORTION:
A Psychiatric View

Formulated by
        the Committee on Psychiatry and Law
GROUP FOR THE ADVANCEMENT OF PSYCHIATRY

CHARLES SCRIBNER'S SONS · NEW YORK

STATEMENT OF PURPOSE

THE GROUP FOR THE ADVANCEMENT OF PSYCHIATRY has a membership of approximately three hundred psychiatrists, most of whom are organized in the form of a number of working committees. These committees direct their efforts toward the study of various aspects of psychiatry and the application of this knowledge to the fields of mental health and human relations.

Collaboration with specialists in other disciplines has been and is one of GAP's working principles. Since the formation of GAP in 1946 its members have worked closely with such other specialists as anthropologists, biologists, economists, statisticians, educators, lawyers, nurses, psychologists, sociologists, social workers, and experts in mass communication,

5

philosophy, and semantics. GAP envisages a continuing program of work according to the following aims:

(1) To collect and appraise significant data in the field of psychiatry, mental health, and human relations;
(2) To re-evaluate old concepts and to develop and test new ones;
(3) To apply the knowledge thus obtained for the promotion of mental health and good human relations.

GAP is an independent group, and its reports represent the composite findings and opinions of its members only, guided by its many consultants.

The Right to Abortion: A Psychiatric View was formulated by the Committee on Psychiatry and Law, whose members are listed at the end of the Preface. Members of all committees of GAP are listed at the end of the book.

CONTENTS

7

8

PREFACE

IN 1966, WHEN THE GAP Committee on Psychiatry and Law first turned its attention to the problem of abortion, the larger segments of the medical and legal fraternities were also beginning to tackle this controversial subject. They approached their task somewhat cautiously, but in the end they emerged in favor of some degree of abortion-law reform. In the summer of 1967 the American Medical Association and the American Psychiatric Association issued position statements supporting modifications in the abortion law similar to those suggested by the American Law Institute (ALI). In September 1967 an International Conference on Abortion was held in Washington, sponsored by the Harvard Divinity School and the Joseph P. Kennedy, Jr., Foundation. Various organizations, notably the Association for the Study of Abortion in New York and The Society for Humane Abortion, Inc., in San Francisco, began to mobilize professional and public sentiment in the direction of a more modern attitude to this age-old problem. In December 1969, two months after the publication of the GAP edition of *The Right to Abortion: A Psychiatric View*, the Board of Trustees of the American Psychiatric Association declared in a resolution that "the decision to have an abortion should be regarded as a medical decision and responsibility," and that criminal penalties "should be reserved for those situations when an abortion is performed by unlicensed or unqualified persons."

Thus, during the intervening three years, the climate of professional and public opinion in regard to abortion has been shifting with astonishing rapidity. These same shifts have even been observed within the tiny microcosm of the Committee. In the early days of its deliberations much of our attention was focused on exploding the myth of the word "therapeutic" when applied to abortion performed on psychiatric grounds. Most of the members of the Committee who favored some "liberalization" of existing laws recoiled from the concept of "abortion on demand" and eyed with suspicion the slightly less charged concept of "abortion on request."

But the more intensively the Committee studied the problem, the more we heard from consultants in sociology and the law, and the more we began to analyze the experience of those states who had "liberalized" their statutes governing abortion, the more we came to recognize that all the liberalization in the world would not help as long as abortion, when performed by a licensed physician, remained within the province of the criminal law. For this and other reasons (described in the text of this report) the Committee concluded that the ALI recommendations were unsatisfactory.

We then became deeply concerned about the plight and the rights of the woman faced with an unwanted and unplanned pregnancy. We discovered that most abortions now performed legally by licensed physicians were performed by stretching the concept of "psychiatric grounds" to the breaking point. Although the psychiatrist may occasionally have a legitimate role in influencing the decision to abort or not to abort, this role is a very limited one.

The Committee was also concerned about the possibility of psychiatric aftereffects in women who had obtained legal abortions. However, no convincing evidence was found to support this fear and considerable evidence to dispel it. We were equally troubled about what happened to the unwanted child born to a mother who had been refused an abortion. Here the evidence showed that a significant percentage of such children later developed psychiatric instability.

Although this report was written from the psychiatric point of view, the religious and moral objections to abortion had to be considered. The Committee concluded that: "For those who take this moral stand [that abortion constitutes murder] there perhaps can be no absolute rebuttal, and certainly those who take this position will themselves avoid abortion and will be shocked by those who condone it." But it is also true that such people do not need the law to support their moral principles. Father Robert F. Drinan, S.J., a noted legal scholar, has stated that he would prefer no law if the alternative was a liberalized law.

The attitude of the courts toward abortion has also been changing rapidly. In September 1969 a decision in the Supreme Court of the State of California (*The People v. Leon*

Phillips Belous; Criminal Case 12739) reversed a conviction for abortion based on an 1850 law. In November 1969 Judge Gerhard A. Gesell of the U.S. District Court for the District of Columbia ruled that the 1901 law which prevented licensed physicians from performing abortions except when "necessary for the preservation of the mother's life or health" was unconstitutional.

These two judicial decisions focus on the ambiguity of the legal phrase "preserving the life of the mother" or "preservation of the life of the mother." This judicial emphasis on the ambiguity of the statutes and the legal questions which derive from that ambiguity as to the rights of both the pregnant woman and the physician may have far-reaching legal effects. These judicial decisions will unquestionably have an impact on subsequent legislative attempts to formulate statutes which meet judicial standards.

After three years of study and debate, the final recommendations of the Committee, later approved by the membership of the Group for the Advancement of Psychiatry, were stated as follows:

". . . We recommend that abortion, when performed by a licensed physician, be entirely removed from the domain of criminal law. We believe that a woman should have the right to abort or not just as she has the right to marry or not."

The Committee is deeply grateful to the two consultants who aided our studies: Alice S. Rossi, Ph.D., Associate Professor, Department of Sociology and Anthropology, Goucher College, Towson, Maryland, who gave generously of her extensive knowledge and whose sociological insights launched us on our way, and Ralph Slovenko, LL.B., Professor of Law, Wayne University Law School, Detroit, Michigan, who provided valuable assistance on the legal aspects of the problem. However, although both these consultants made important contributions, the Committee assumes full responsibility for the final version of this report and is solely responsible for any errors of fact or opinion.

COMMITTEE ON PSYCHIATRY AND LAW
GROUP FOR THE ADVANCEMENT OF PSYCHIATRY

Zigmond M. Lebensohn, M.D., Chairman
Edward T. Auer, M.D.
John Donnelly, M.D.
Jay Katz, M.D.
Carl M. Malmquist, M.D.
Seymour Pollack, M.D.
Alan A. Stone, M.D.
Gene L. Usdin, M.D.
Andrew S. Watson, M.D.

THE RIGHT TO ABORTION:

A Psychiatric View

INTRODUCTION

DURING THE PAST TWO DECADES there has been an increasing
tendency to invoke the psychiatrist as the arbiter at critical
points of conflict between existing social policy and individual dissent and disagreement; abortion is one such instance of
this tendency. Psychiatrists do have a relevant contribution
to make to a resolution of the abortion dilemma, but their
contribution is limited. When the psychiatrist serves as the
deus ex machina of the conflicted social system, he may ease
the immediate stress without clarifying or resolving the
underlying divisiveness of the community. The unfortunate
consequences of this are that society places undue responsibility upon the individual psychiatrist and at the same time
shuns its own responsibility to face squarely the serious and
sometimes critical issues that have led to such divisiveness.
Because of these considerations and because the regulation of

access to abortion is, in fact, the product of religious, moral, ethical, socioeconomic, political, and legal considerations, in what follows psychiatric factors are examined in relation to these broader perspectives.

one | # THE OBLIGATIONS OF MOTHERHOOD

MOTHERING IS A TASK that requires enormous human and emotional resources. It is an obligation that confronts and challenges the woman's capacity to care night and day. When this task is carried out in the spirit of love and fulfillment, it is hard but rewarding work. But when the child is unwanted, the task may become onerous, and the obligations created may become a lifetime sentence, an ordeal emotionally destructive to the mother and disastrous for the child. Despite these serious psychological consequences, motherhood is so universally revered as a natural fulfillment of the life cycle and as a sacred obligation to the potential of a new life that once the woman becomes pregnant, we tend to ignore the element of choice or to condemn those who in a variety of situations would choose abortion. It is out of this social, religious, and psychological climate that laws regulating abortion have been drawn. In addition, some writers have emphasized the "masculinist" aspect of this climate as central to a proper psychological understanding of the law.

Abortion laws as currently enacted[1] (including those "liberalized" under the American Law Institute's Model Statute[2]) require virtually all women, married or single, old or young, to carry the fetus to term and as a consequence in many instances to serve a lifetime sentence.[3] The married woman who becomes pregnant by inadvertence, the young girl who becomes pregnant out of inexperience, the promiscuous woman who becomes pregnant out of indiscretion are all subject to this same sentence. Once the error has been made, none of these women has the right to control her own fate unless she can prove to doctors that her mental or physical health is in danger.[4] In some states abortion is allowed only when the mother's death is imminent.[5]

A society desperately in need of population and manpower perhaps might expect its women to make this sacrifice. But Western society today, on the contrary, is threatened by overpopulation.[6] Yet women are legally forced to fulfill a biological function that, when it is unwanted, has no rational justification from this perspective of the state. No abortion statute (except perhaps that of Japan[7]) takes into account the specific problem of overpopulation. Such a statute would suggest recognition and legitimization of the fact that abortion constitutes a secondary means of "contraception" and planned motherhood in an overpopulated society.

two

RELIGIOUS AND MORAL
OBJECTIONS TO ABORTION

THERE CAN BE NO DOUBT that strong religious ideals con-
tribute to sustaining the system of legal sanctions that makes
abortion a source of guilt and labels it a crime.[1] Thus, in
Roman Catholic doctrine, as the legal scholar Father
Robert F. Drinan, S.J., states, "An abortion is the taking of
the life of an unborn but, nevertheless, a real human being."
However, he argues that traditional abortion law is not
simply the translation of "the views of his religion into the
civil law . . . to impose them on others." He defends this
view by various arguments from constitutional and criminal
law but concedes that the Judeo-Christian religious tradition
"in fact is probably the principal source of Anglo-American
law . . . which regulates conduct deemed to constitute a
crime against society."[2] In contrast, the American Civil
Liberties Union questions the constitutionality of abortion
laws on the ground that such laws "are possibly violative of
the First Amendment clause forbidding the establishment of

religion [by the state] and guaranteeing the separation of church and state.[3]

Basic to Father Drinan's view is the concept (shared by theologians of many religious persuasions) of the "inviolability of every human life" and the Roman Catholic dictum that the embryo should from the moment of conception be considered a human life. However, we should point out that, in the course of history, both the Roman Catholic Church and English law have altered their judgments as to the time at which the embryo should be considered a human life.[4] For centuries, in both English law and Roman Catholic dogma, abortion was not considered to have occurred unless the fetus had quickened.* At the very least, this suggests that the religious definition of abortion has not always been precise. Indeed, many people and some religious groups currently *do not* consider abortion before quickening the equivalent of murder.[5] Religious attitudes toward abortion are also deeply influenced by considerations of when the soul begins as contrasted with potentially demonstrable definitions of when life begins.

Even our abortion laws as they now are applied and our technological advances in birth control betray a basic equivocation regarding the question of abortion and the implicit moral issues of "when life begins" and what constitutes the "taking of a life." Were our society convinced that abortion is murder, it would exact the same penalty against abortionists as is levied against other parties to premeditated murder

* Quickening is the first recognizable movement of the fetus *in utero*, appearing from the fourth to the fifth month of pregnancy.

—life imprisonment or even capital punishment. Of course our society does no such thing; for example, the punishment prescribed for criminal abortion in California is a sentence of two to five years in a state prison.[6] Moreover, as Garrett Hardin pointed out, "If abortion is a crime, then the woman who aborts is certainly a criminal. . . . If a crime, it is a most remarkable one in that it is the only crime for which we prosecute the accessories to the crime and never the principal herself." [7]

Just as the curious application of the criminal law itself indicates ambiguity and doubt in our attitudes about abortion, so does our reaction to technological progress in developing methods of birth control. The "loop" or intra-uterine device (IUD) and the experimental "morning after" pills prevent development of the fetus by halting the implantation of the fertilized egg in the uterine wall. Some authorities flatly contend that in the case of the IUD a spontaneous abortion takes place a few weeks after implantation. At any rate, the function of these chemical and mechanical means of birth control is probably to interrupt the pregnancy *after* conception has taken place.* In so doing, these contraceptives have made it all the more difficult to draw the line between contraception and abortion. Perhaps the fact that no legal authorities are really concerned as to whether such devices are, in fact, abortifacients casts further doubt on the wisdom of attempting to bind all members of our society to a mono-

---

* There is, however, a minority view that the IUD interferes with the movement of the sperm and thus prevents conception from taking place.

lithic judgment that regards any form of abortion as murder. In these circumstances the 1965 Supreme Court ruling (*Griswold v. Connecticut*, 381 U.S. 479) holding unconstitutional a state law against a married couple's use of contraceptives takes on increasing significance and may in the future be brought to bear on abortion as well. Father Drinan has specially objected to such a possible interpretation of this ruling.[8]

As psychiatrists we fully recognize that for some women the sanctity of motherhood comes from a combination of religious belief and a sense of personal fulfillment. We also recognize that for other women the sanctity of motherhood derives *solely* from the sense of personal or marital fulfillment. Even if this latter group were a small minority, their choice about motherhood ought not be bound by the religious convictions of the majority. This established principle suggests that to the extent the law does translate secular and religious values into criminal sanction, some legal justification might be found not only for permitting these women to obtain abortion, but for permitting them to obtain it with dignity and privacy and without public stigma.

Despite the foregoing considerations, many will argue as does Father Drinan that abortion constitutes murder and/or that it violates the rights of the unborn embryo. For those who take this moral stand there perhaps can be no absolute rebuttal, and certainly those who take this position will themselves avoid abortion and will be shocked by those who condone it.

It is important to add that some Roman Catholic authorities have indicated that they, too, believe that specific law is not needed to support specific Roman Catholic principle. Thus, Cardinal Cushing of Boston is quoted as saying that Catholics do not need the law to support their moral principles.[9] Father Drinan has stated that he would prefer no law if the alternative was to be a liberalized law.[10]

three | THE RIGHTS OF THE WOMAN

AGAINST THE SEEMINGLY INSOLUBLE PROBLEMS presented by the "moral issue" of abortion, we must balance the consideration owed to the basic tenet of a democratic society—that people should be permitted to exercise a maximum degree of individual freedom, bound only by a proper regard for the legitimate rights of other citizens. We submit that, under the current system of law, by denying a woman the right to rectify error through the process of abortion, our statutes stand foursquare against her right to control her own reproductive life.

A particularly repugnant feature of current practice is that the economically affluent do not find it difficult to procure a "therapeutic" abortion. Thus, it is amply clear that a majority of "therapeutic" abortions are performed on private as opposed to clinic patients.[1] For example, one study found twenty times more private than clinic cases.[2] Similarly, the wealthy can afford the high fees charged by most of those competent practitioners who are willing to take the risks of performing an illegal abortion. Furthermore, there are a number of places in the world where a woman can readily obtain an abortion if she can afford the trip. Bulgaria, Czechoslovakia, Denmark, England, Finland, Hungary, Iceland, Japan, Norway, Poland, Sweden, U.S.S.R., and Yugoslavia, under varying circumstances, authorize abortions on terms substantially more liberal than those found in the United States.[3] Thus, our laws do not effectively prohibit abortion for the affluent.

The American Civil Liberties Union in 1967 took the position that current abortion laws "deny the women in lower economic groups the equal protection of the laws guaranteed by the Fourteenth Amendment, since abortions are now freely available to the rich but forbidden to the poor." The ACLU stated: "It should not be deemed a crime for a woman to seek, and for a doctor to perform, the termination of a pregnancy in accordance with generally accepted community standards of medical practice. The ACLU believes that all criminal sanctions should be removed from the area of abortion, and that the laws and standards governing this medical procedure be the same as those which govern the performance of all medical procedures. The Union views present abortion laws as unconstitutional because:

(1)   They are unconstitutionally vague;
(2)   They deny to women in lower economic groups the equal protection of the laws guaranteed by the Fourteenth Amendment, since abortions are now

freely available to the rich but forbidden to the poor;

(3)   They infringe the constitutional right to decide whether and when to have a child, as well as the marital right of privacy and the privacy of the relationship between patient and physician;

(4)   They impair the constitutional right of physicians to practice in accordance with their professional obligations, in that they require doctors to refrain from a medical procedure whose failure to perform would, except for the abortion laws, amount to malpractice in many cases, and

(5)   They deprive women of their lives and liberty, in the sense of deciding how their bodies are to be used, without due process of law." [4]

Those who cannot afford the high fees of competent abortionists are driven by their need into the hands of unscrupulous practitioners and charlatans who may employ dangerous techniques for inducing abortion. It is within this large sector of the population that the unnecessary deaths and complications resulting from incompetence occur.[5] Known deaths from abortions in the United States in 1965 totaled 235 women, of whom 106 were white and 129 nonwhite. In addition to the serious dangers of the procedures under these circumstances, women in this situation must suffer emotional experiences hardly to be surpassed for their sordid, demeaning, and shame-inducing character.[6] It can be said, then, that current laws as enforced have in fact done little to alter the large number of criminal and illegal abortions carried out in our society. Although statistics for the United States can be challenged, the data suggest a minimum of 100,000 abortions a year, and some estimates indicate there may be more than a million.[7] If the maximum estimate should prove correct, this would mean that one embryo is aborted for every four children who are born. Whichever estimate is correct, unquestionably the vast majority of these abortions are illegal and therefore not performed under optimal medical or psychological conditions. Thus, decisions are made individually and personally, responsive to social, economic, moral, religious, and psychological factors, regardless of the status of the law. The noted psychoanalyst Helene Deutsch has commented on this aspect of the problem as follows:

"Public opinion, common sense, and normal moral judgment supports the woman's human right to be a mother or to avoid being a mother by any of the means at her disposal according to her wishes. . . . The normal emotional reaction to abortion is overwhelmingly in the most varied civilizations to take the woman's part despite any laws to the contrary."[8]

four	# THE UNWANTED CHILD

THE PREDICAMENT OF THE FUTURE CHILD, should he be born, also cannot be ignored. More systematic research in this area is badly needed, but one significant study has been carried out in Sweden with 120 children born after applications for a therapeutic abortion had been refused. These children, born during the 1939–1941 period, were followed up until age twenty-one for assessment in terms of mental health, social adjustment, and educational level. They were compared to a control group composed of the very next child of the same sex born at the same hospital or in the same district to a different mother. The mothers of the control group were not selected on the basis of their maturity but simply by the criteria of proximity in time, in geography, and in the sex of offspring. The results of this study indicated that: "The unwanted children were worse off in every respect. . . . The differences were often significant [statistically] and when they were not, they pointed in the same

direction . . . to a worse lot for the unwanted child." [1]
This is certainly not unexpected, since the adverse consequences of maternal rejection have long been recognized
by psychiatrists as one of the major contributing elements of
human psychopathology.[2] In fact, some psychiatrists believe
that one of the most important goals of preventive psychiatry
is the prevention of "unwanted offspring"; such prevention
was declared by Dr. Stephen Fleck to be "preventive psychiatry's single most effective tool." [3]

Surely, in the face of the population explosion, society
no longer has a need to compel the birth of such unwanted
children. To the contrary, an informed and timely social
policy should emphasize that for the sake of the family as
well as of society such children as are born should be
wanted. Stressing this point, Hardin referred to the positive
aspect of abortion:

"Critics of abortion generally see it as an exclusively
negative thing, a means of nonfulfillment only. What they
fail to realize is that abortion, like other means of birth
control, can lead to fulfillment in the life of a woman. A
woman who aborts this year because she is in poor health,
neurotic, economically harassed, unmarried, on the verge of
divorce, or immature may well decide to have some other
child five years from now—a wanted child. If her need for
abortion is frustrated she may never know the joy of a
wanted child." [4]

This observation takes on special significance in light
of the increasing ability of doctors to diagnose serious
genetic defects in the third and fourth months of pregnancy.

In a recently reported instance, such a diagnosis led to a therapeutic abortion of a fetus certain to develop into a child requiring life-long institutional care and allowed the mother to deliver a normal child in a subsequent pregnancy.[5]

five | SOME TABOOS AND
MISLEADING ASSUMPTIONS

WHILE MANY OTHER social, moral, and pragmatic goals may be offered as rationale for retaining the sanctions against abortion, our observation suggests that the historical and scientific developments of the past two decades have attenuated many of these factors. Some examples will illustrate this.

In the past, the threat or fear of pregnancy supported our society's taboos about virginity. Whether or not one supports strict sexual sanctions, the widespread availability of chemical and mechanical contraceptives has already eroded this traditional fear of pregnancy in many segments of society. Threat of pregnancy as a support of sexual morality and virginity has therefore lost some of its deterrent effect. Furthermore, we would suggest that the psychological cost of unwanted children far outweighs the limited gain in sexual morality that results from the fear of pregnancy.

While abortion at one time constituted a serious surgical procedure, involving considerable morbidity and some death, modern surgical techniques together with antibiotics have minimized these risks. A vacuum evacuation procedure has been developed which has already reduced morbidity and mortality to the status of insignificant factors. This procedure has been found to compare favorably with the conventional use of curettage in respect to loss of blood and both early and later complications.[1] Hardin has pointed out that in Hungary, where legal abortion is readily available (and where the vacuum technique has been introduced), the death rate in more than a quarter of a million cases is less than 6 per 100,000. This contrasts with U.S. statistics of 17 deaths per 100,000 resulting from the removal of tonsils and adenoids and 24 deaths per 100,000 resulting from childbirth and its complications.[2] Finally, the advent of a new class of risk-free abortifacient drugs can potentially make the interruption of pregnancy a nonsurgical procedure. This would mean that every practicing physician, on a simple prescriptive basis, would be able to terminate pregnancy harmlessly within the early phase of gestation.

These developments make it clear that the physical risk to the pregnant woman is so small as to be negligible today and will be still less in the future. It is, therefore, even more tragic that many American women are forced to seek criminal abortions wherein the risk of morbidity and mortality is relatively high.

An opinion frequently proffered by both medical and nonmedical authorities argues that a woman who aborts undergoes adverse psychological aftereffects.[3] One typical view holds that the normal psychophysiological depression which ensues on the interruption of pregnancy combines with a feeling of guilt to produce a focal point for future depressive episodes and that abortion may even in some cases precipitate psychosis or serious neurosis. The published evidence dealing with this supposed deleterious impact of abortion has been summarized by Nathan M. Simon and Audrey G. Senturia and meticulously reviewed by Dr. R. Bruce Sloane.[4] Sloane concluded that the earlier findings of serious and lasting psychiatric disturbance are:

(1)   often based on a statistically biased self-selection of subjects or are simply case studies without efforts to standardize the sample or balance it against a control group[5];

(2)   inadequately differentiated as to pre-existing conditions and abortion sequelae;

(3)   highly variable (in one study, for example, 43 percent of aborted women showed moderate to severe guilt, while in another study none of the women could be so designated).[6]

Furthermore, recent more careful studies of cases made by Simon and others suggest that women who in psychiatric terms are relatively normal respond to abortion with only a mild and self-limited depression without lasting psychological disturbance. Psychiatrically disturbed women who undergo abortion for the most part remain stabilized or even improve. Simon's excellent retrospective study on women who were therapeutically aborted concludes: "Our study did

35

not produce support for the frequently expressed belief that therapeutic abortion results in involuntary infertility, difficulty in sexual relations, or is a precipitant in involutional depression." [7]

Thus, the dire predictions of dangerous aftereffects that had become embedded in medical teaching have not been fulfilled in controlled clinical studies or in our own clinical experience, particularly if the woman was strongly motivated in her desire for an abortion. There are exceptions, of course, but the most notable of these seem to occur when the woman becomes sterile as a consequence of infection at the time of the abortion.[8] The sterility means she can never replace her loss by attaining motherhood in more gratifying circumstances. Since this occurs most often in nonmedical, illegal abortion, its significance could be markedly reduced if abortion were legalized.

Finally, during the 1950s it had been quite difficult for couples who were themselves sterile to adopt children. It had been an era of black-market babies, of long waiting and stringent selection of adoptive parents. The past few years have brought a reversal in this trend; in many urban areas it is currently impossible to find adequate adopting parents for unwanted infants. Out of an estimated total of three million illegitimate children under eighteen years of age in the United States in December 1961, 31 percent had been adopted; statistics by race show that while 26 percent of such white children had found adopting parents, only 5 percent of the nonwhites had.[9] The woman who continues the pregnancy of an unwanted child in the hope of finding adopting parents for her baby is very likely to be disappointed. Thus, this justification for requiring the unwilling mother to lend her body to the continued obligation of pregnancy has also diminished.

six | THE AMERICAN LAW INSTITUTE'S "LIBERALIZED" ABORTION LAW

THE PROTAGONISTS FOR REFORM of abortion laws have generally embraced the proposals of the American Law Institute:

"A licensed physician is justified in terminating a pregnancy if:

(1)   He believes that there is substantial risk that continuance of the pregnancy would gravely impair the physical or mental health of the mother or that the child would be born with grave physical or mental defect, or the pregnancy resulted from rape by force or its equivalent . . . or from incest . . . ; and

(2)   Two physicians, one of whom may be the person performing the abortion, have certified in writing their belief in the justifying circumstances, and have filed such certificate prior to the abortion in the licensed hospital where it was to be performed,

or in such other place as may be designated by law." [1]

For a number of reasons we find the ALI proposals unsatisfactory.

First, for those insistent upon developing a statute that provides a social "resolution" of the moral issues, the ALI proposal is clearly of no help. For those convinced that abortion is murder, the ALI statute is nothing but a broadened license for professionals to authorize murders. (Father Drinan takes the position that the ALI proposal "seeks to evade the basic question of whether the fetus has a right to be born." While opposed to abortion except where it is necessary to save the life of the mother, he notes that an absence of law with respect to abortion "has at least the merit of not involving the law and society in the business of selecting those persons whose lives may be legally terminated. A system of permitting abortion on request has the undeniable virtue of neutralizing the law so that, while the law does not forbid abortion, it does not on the other hand sanction it—even on a presumably restricted basis." [2])

For those convinced, as we are, that the moral issues present an insoluble dilemma that should be left to individual conscience rather than be the subject of a social policy judgment, the ALI proposal disregards the right of a woman to control her own life.

A second objection applies specifically to the extent of the role assigned psychiatrists. In an effort to liberalize the law in this field, the ALI proposal makes provision for abortion where a psychiatrist has found "substantial risk" that continuance of the pregnancy would gravely impair the mental health of the woman. Some legal criticism suggests that these "medico-legal standards" of "substantial risk," "gravely impair," and even "mental health" defy objective or consistent interpretations. David W. Louisell argues that there is "nothing in the statute which would aid the physician in making the determination. At the very least the statutory language provides a fertile ground for the application of individual subjective notions. . . ." [3]

There are indeed studies that suggest that this criticism is just and that it applies to statutes in existence for many years as well as to the ALI. Thus we find that the rate of therapeutic abortion varies dramatically from hospital to hospital within a state, even though all are supposedly governed by the same statutes.[4] There is also variation in specific interpretation of the statute by different psychiatrists, as demonstrated in several questionnaire studies.[5] Although differing hospital policies explain some of the variations in abortion rates, the reports that demonstrate the wide variation in psychiatric opinion as to which pregnant women conform to the standards of the statute raise serious doubts about the reliability of psychiatric determinations.

The crucial question to be answered is: Are there psychiatric criteria that can be consistently and validly applied in the face of an ambiguous medico-legal standard?

Consistency is used here in a simple statistical sense—that is, are there criteria that different experts will be able to apply in an objective and systematic fashion, or that the same expert will be able to apply objectively and systematically on different occasions? An assessment of the consistency of psychiatric criteria must include some consideration of such matters as the inherent ambiguity of the relevant clinical phenomena to be described, the extent to which psychiatric as distinct from legal criteria leave wide discretionary powers to the psychiatrist, and so forth. Validity is also used in a statistical sense—that is, are there in fact data suggesting that psychiatric criteria, when consistently applied, can successfully predict grave impairment of a woman's mental health by her continued pregnancy and childbirth? This distinction between consistency and validity is meant to emphasize that even if psychiatrists of diverse background and training could rate patients for abortion in a consistent way, it still might be true that abortion is in fact beneficial to all or to none of the women who request it, no matter how they are rated.

We shall first consider the question of consistency. The following circumscribed and traditional criteria, although infrequently encountered, could probably be consistently applied by different psychiatrists when consulted on the advisability of abortion:

(1)   Previous pregnancies have repeatedly precipitated post-partum psychotic reactions.

(2)   The mother has previously undergone lobotomy.

(3)   The mother is a clear-cut "process" schizophrenic

or is in the throes of an acute schizophrenic episode.

(4)   The mother has a severe and recurrent affective disorder.

(5)   There are profound suicidal or homicidal tendencies.

A second group of criteria are more ambiguous, but far more often used by psychiatrists to characterize women requesting abortion:

(1)   The presence of mild suicidal ideation or suicidal gestures in a woman who might be treated by brief hospitalization or outpatient care.

(2)   Symptoms of mild neurosis or characterological problems.

(3)   Situations where the mother shows pronounced emotional or intellectual immaturity and is likely to be incapable of raising her child or coping with motherhood.

(4)   A broad range of socioeconomic factors that create serious psychological hardship for the mother.[7]

Almost any woman who wants an abortion might fit into this second set of criteria and thus might be considered by some psychiatrists as meeting the medico-legal standard of "substantial risk" to "mental health." However, it should be noted that, although the risk of suicide is one of the commonest reasons for allowing abortion, Sloane's findings suggest that actual suicide in these circumstances is rare.[8]

Patients who fit the first set of criteria are in a minority of those requesting abortion, but even in such easily distinguished cases as these the validity of the "therapeutic indication" is disputable.

The major question of *valid* psychiatric therapeutic indication to be decided is: Will the abortion and *its* effects be more traumatic than pregnancy, childbirth, and forced motherhood? Since our predictive criteria rarely foretell with any certainty what happens to the mother when abortion is denied, they have little if any proven validity. Indeed, in the opinion of Dr. Myre Sim, a British psychiatrist, "There are no psychiatric grounds for termination of pregnancy," and the psychiatrist "has no factual basis for being associated with the problem." [9]

Sloane has been only slightly less categorical: "There are no unequivocal psychiatric indications for therapeutic abortion." Dr. Sloane's judgment is that "the risk of exacerbation or precipitation of a psychosis is small and *unpredictable*, and suicide [is] rare." [10]

Most often the psychiatrist finds psychodynamic considerations that are in conflict in this matter. [11] Which side of the ambivalence he chooses to support may well be based on some unarticulated moral, social, or policy judgment rather than on individual clinical considerations. Thus we agree with Dr. Joseph Rheingold in questioning the propriety of calling upon individual psychiatrists to be the ultimate decision makers on behalf of society. Dr. Rheingold has written:

"The explanation of the inconsistency of attitude [on the part of psychiatrists] lies both in the psychiatrist himself and in the complexity of the situations under judgment.

43

Apart from his religious convictions, the psychiatrist is influenced by his ethical and philosophical leanings, his social values, his professional associations, and the abortion 'taboo' among physicians, the pressures put upon him and his unconscious dispositions. The methodological approach, too, is variable. . . . The psychiatrist may or may not take into account humanitarian factors, the socioeconomic situation, the woman's significant relationships, eugenic possibilities, and the quality of prospective motherhood. He may conform to the letter of the law, he may allow himself a very liberal interpretation of it, or in good faith, he may use subterfuge to bring his findings into consonance with the law. . . . He may err in either direction: The woman may be aborted, with regrettable consequence, or she may not be aborted, with regrettable consequences." [12]

Doubtless many psychiatrists will continue to work within the ALI and similar current legal systems in the hope of helping individual patients who want an abortion. However, we believe it essential that psychiatrists, through their professional associations, begin to recognize their own limitations and back away from the invitation to accept responsibility for making decisions that more appropriately rest in the broader community. Although we cannot agree with the categorical nature of Dr. Sim's judgment, his words go to the heart of the issue: "If society wants abortion to be easier, it should have the courage to campaign for it honestly and not exploit the psychiatrist. . . ." [13]

An unfortunate consequence of the specific psychiatric

the time and bother of justifying an abortion before a reviewing committee." [18]

Finally, the ALI statute also allows abortion when the child would be born with grave physical or mental defect and when the pregnancy results from rape, incest, or felonious intercourse. The former ground permits "eugenic considerations not hitherto known in American law." [19] The latter ground creates the problem of rapid determination of the factual elements of rape and incest. In both instances, major psychological, social, genetic, and legal questions are left unanswered.

seven

RECOMMENDATIONS

MANY OF THE social, sexual, and pragmatic aims that were advanced by legal sanctions against abortion have diminished in significance in recent years. Their continued application no longer can be sustained by a justifiable state interest. If anything, it may be in the interest of the state to permit abortion freely as a secondary measure to limit population where contraception fails. The laws as currently enforced impose an enormous hardship on the unwilling mother, whatever her medical or psychiatric condition may be.

There remains the moral issue of abortion as murder. We submit that this is insoluble—a matter of religious philosophy and religious principle and not a matter of fact. We suggest that those who believe abortion is murder need not avail themselves of it. On the other hand, we do not believe that the existence of this belief should limit the freedom of those not bound by identical religious conviction. Although the moral issue hangs like a threatening cloud over any open discussion of abortion, the moral issues are not all one-sided. The psychoanalyst Erik H. Erikson stated the other side well when he suggested, "The most deadly of all possible sins is the mutilation of a child's spirit." [1] There can be nothing more destructive to a child's spirit than being unwanted, and there are few things more disruptive to a woman's spirit than being forced into motherhood without love or need.

On the basis of the foregoing discussion we recommend that abortion, when performed by a licensed physician, be entirely removed from the domain of criminal law. We believe that a woman should have the right to abort or not, just as she has the right to marry or not. This position is shared by a number of other groups, notably the President's Task Force.[2]

We suggest that the physician who is asked to perform the abortion be expected to exercise medical judgment as he would in the case of any elective surgery. Medical judgment will be affected by many factors. Perhaps the most controversial of these will be the length of gestation and the viability of the fetus. However, we believe that general rather than specific guidelines should be instituted. Thus, we assume that most physicians, as gestation progresses, will be increasingly reluctant to perform abortion.

The physician should have the right to refuse to perform abortion on the basis of his own moral or religious convictions. Protection for the operating surgeon against any legal claim of the father is also essential. It has been argued that a policy that places primary emphasis on the woman's right to control her own reproductive life neglects the right of the husband to become a father.[3] In fact, a recent California decision raised the possibility that the husband has a legal cause of action and that he can sue for damages the doctor who aborts his wife over his (the husband's) wishes.[4] Such a legal principle, if widely applied, would undoubtedly lead to a routine requirement of joint consent. While it is difficult to predict how often such conflict may occur, the possibility suggests that the physician who elects to perform an abortion should consider consulting in advance with both husband and wife. There may, however, be instances when abortion is desired and the husband is not the father; therefore a standard regulation that requires the husband's consent might infringe on the woman's privacy. Similarly, a wife's exercise of her right to abort could become a ground for divorce by a husband who wishes his marriage consummated by children. These countervailing rights of wife and husband remain problematic.

As psychiatrists we would particularly emphasize the importance of the physician's exploring with the pregnant woman the basis of her motivation, so as to clarify impulsive, manipulative, or self-destructive elements in the decision to abort. The various medical judgments pertinent to abortion may, when warranted, be arrived at with the help of consultation. We do not believe that psychiatric consultation should necessarily be routine.

We are well aware that our recommendations constitute a broad change of social policy. Given the experiences in some of the East European countries, where liberalized abortion laws produced a major decline in population growth,[5] we recommend that the Bureau of Census, the various population centers, and the various social and psychological research centers study the consequences of this change and, where indicated, recommend future changes. What we suggest is not necessarily a final step, but rather a currently appropriate measure.

REFERENCE NOTES

REFERENCE NOTES

chapter one • THE OBLIGATIONS OF MOTHERHOOD

1. For a review of existing state abortion laws, see U.S. Department of Labor, *Report of the Task Force on Family Law and Policy to the Citizen's Advisory Council on the Status of Women* (Government Publication No. Y3.IN8/21:2F21, 1968), pp. 28–29; also B. J. George, Jr., "Current Abortion Laws; Proposals and Movements for Reform," pp. 1–36, and Kenneth R. Niswander, "Medical Abortion Practices in the United States," in David T. Smith (ed.), *Abortion and the Law*, pp. 37–59 (Cleveland: Press of Case–Western Reserve University, 1967).
2. ALI Model Penal Code, 207.11 (2).
3. Robert E. Cooke *et al.* (eds.), *The Terrible Choice: The Abortion Dilemma* (For the Joseph P. Kennedy, Jr., Foundation; New York: Bantam Books, 1968), Chapter 2, "Five Case Studies," pp. 5–33. Under prevailing abortion laws in most states, none of the women in the five representative case studies described would be allowed to obtain a legal abortion.
4. See Alice S. Rossi (Department of Social Relations, Johns Hopkins University), "Social Change and Abortion Law Re-

form" (unpublished paper presented to the American Orthopsychiatric Association, Chicago, March 21, 1968); also Garrett Hardin, "Abortion and Human Dignity" (public lecture given at the University of California at Berkeley, April 29, 1964; San Francisco: The Citizens Committee for Humane Abortion Laws); U.S. Department of Labor, *Report on Family Law*, p. 31.

5. Smith, *Abortion and the Law*, pp. 37–59, lists states that permit abortion only to save the life of the mother and discusses their laws.
6. Kingsley Davis, "Population Policy: Will Current Programs Succeed?" *Science*, Vol. 158, No. 3802 (1967), pp. 730–739.
7. Smith, *Abortion and the Law*, p. 4.

chapter two • RELIGIOUS AND MORAL OBJECTIONS
TO ABORTION

1. See R. Curran, "The Quiet Murder," *Linacre Quarterly*, November 1966, pp. 344–348.
2. Robert F. Drinan, "Abortion and the Law," in Smith, *Abortion and the Law*, pp. 108 and 122.
3. Cooke, *The Terrible Choice*, p. 96.
4. Glanville Williams, *The Sanctity of Life and the Criminal Law* (New York: Knopf, 1957), pp. 148–183. See also R. Huser, *The Crime of Abortion in Canon Law, An Historical Synopsis and Commentary*. (Washington, D.C.: The Catholic University of America Press, 1942).
5. See, for example, the reports of the 16th Annual Convention of American Baptists and the 1968 General Assembly of Unitarian Universalists, *Newsletter of the Association for the Study of Abortion*, Vol. III, No. 3 (Fall 1968).
6. See Roy Lucas, "Federal Constitutional Limitations on the Enforcement and Administration of State Abortion Statutes," *North Carolina Law Review*, Vol. 46, 1967–68, pp. 730–738,

for the various state penalties for criminal abortion and the state statutes of abortion.

7. Hardin, "Abortion and Human Dignity."
8. Drinan, "The Inviolability of the Right to be Born," in Smith, *Abortion and the Law*, pp. 107–123.
9. Smith, *Abortion and the Law*, p. 56.
10. Harvard Law School Forum, 1967.

chapter three • THE RIGHTS OF THE WOMAN

1. Robert E. Hall, "Therapeutic Abortion, Sterilization, and Contraception," *American Journal of Obstetrics and Gynecology*, Vol. 91 (1965), pp. 518–532.
2. Kenneth R. Niswander *et al.*, "Changing Attitudes Toward Therapeutic Abortion," *Journal of the American Medical Association*, Vol. 196 (1966), pp. 1140–1143; and Sophia J. Kleegman, "Planned Parenthood: Its Influence on Public Health and Family Welfare," in Harold Rosen (ed.), *Therapeutic Abortion: Medical, Psychiatric, Legal, Anthropological, and Religious Considerations*. (New York: The Julian Press, 1954), pp. 254–265.
3. See Ruth Roemer, "Abortion Law: The Approaches of Different Nations," *American Journal of Public Health*, Vol. 57 (1967), pp. 1906–1922, for a review of the laws governing abortions in various countries.
4. American Civil Liberties Union Policy Guide, revised October, 1967.
5. Cooke, *The Terrible Choice*, p. 47.
6. See Philip Roth, *Letting Go* (New York: Random House, 1962), for a moving literary description of this emotional experience.
7. R. Bruce Sloane, "The Unwanted Pregnancy," *New England Journal of Medicine*, Vol. 280 (1969), pp. 1206–1213.
8. Helene Deutsch, *Psychology of Women*: Vol. 2, *Motherhood*. (London: Research Books, 1947), p. 165.

chapter four • THE UNWANTED CHILD

1. Hans Forssman and Inga Thuwe, "One Hundred and Twenty Children Born After Application for Therapeutic Abortion Refused," *Acta Psychiatrica Scandinavica*, Vol. 42 (1966), pp. 71–88. See also Gerald Caplan, "The Disturbance of the Mother-Child Relationship by Unsuccessful Attempts at Abortion," *Mental Hygiene*, Vol. 38 (1954), pp. 67–80.
2. John Bowlby, *Maternal Deprivation* (New York: Schocken Books, 1966).
3. Stephen Fleck, M.D., "Some Psychiatric Aspects of Abortion" (unpublished paper presented to the Connecticut Medical Society, May 2, 1968).
4. Hardin, "Abortion and Human Dignity," p. 5.
5. *Boston Globe*, October 16, 1968, p. 3.

chapter five • SOME TABOOS AND MISLEADING ASSUMPTIONS

1. Emil Vladov, "The Vacuum Aspiration Method for Interruption of Early Pregnancy," *American Journal of Obstetrics and Gynecology*, Vol. 99 (1967), pp. 202–207.
2. Hardin, "Abortion and Human Dignity," p. 1.
3. May Romm, "Psychoanalytic Considerations in Therapeutic Abortion," in Rosen, *Therapeutic Abortion*.
4. Nathan M. Simon and Audrey G. Senturia, "Psychiatric Sequelae of Abortion: Review of the Literature 1935–64," *Archives of General Psychiatry*, Vol. 15 (1966), p. 378; Sloane, "The Unwanted Pregnancy."
5. Frederick J. Taussig, *Abortion, Spontaneous and Induced: Medical and Social Aspects* (St. Louis: C. V. Mosby Co., 1936).
6. See in Mary S. Calderone, (ed.), *Abortion in the United States* (New York: Hoeber–Harper, 1958), pp. 133–136, Bard Brekke, "Other Aspects of Abortion Problems."

7. Nathan M. Simon, Audrey G. Senturia, and David Rothman, "Psychiatric Illness Following Therapeutic Abortion," *American Journal of Psychiatry*, Vol. 124 (1967), pp. 59–65. See also Arthur Peck and Harold Marcus, "Psychiatric Sequelae of Therapeutic Interruption of Pregnancy," *Journal of Nervous and Mental Disease*, Vol. 143 (1966), pp. 417–425; Jerome M. Kummer, "Post-Abortion Psychiatric Illness—A Myth?" *American Journal of Psychiatry*, Vol. 119 (1963), pp. 980–983; Martin Ekblad, "Induced Abortion on Psychiatric Grounds: A Follow-up Study of 479 Women," *Acta Psychiatrica et Neurologica Scandinavica*, Supp. 99 (1955), and Fleck, "Some Psychiatric Effects of Abortion."
8. Deutsch, *Psychology of Women*, Vol. 2, p. 165.
9. Caleb Foote *et al.*, *Cases and Materials on Family Law* (Boston: Little, Brown, 1966), p. 88.

chapter six • THE AMERICAN LAW INSTITUTE'S "LIBERALIZED" ABORTION LAW

1. ALI Model Penal Code, Sections 207.4(1); 207.3.
2. Robert F. Drinan, "The Right of the Fetus to Be Born" (unpublished paper prepared for the International Conference on Abortion, Washington, D.C., September 6–8, 1967). See also J. Lynch, "A Report: Legalized Abortion," and N. Camardese, "Man Plays God" (editorial), *Linacre Quarterly*, Vol. 35, No. 1 (1968), pp. 39–41, 42.
3. David W. Louisell, "Abortion, the Practice of Medicine and the Due Process of Law," *UCLA Law Review*, Vol. 16, No. 2 (1969), pp. 233–254.
4. Keith Russell, "Changing Indications for Therapeutic Abortion: Twenty Years' Experience at Los Angeles County Hospital," *Journal of the American Medical Association*, Vol. 151 (1953), p. 108; Herbert L. Packer and Ralph J. Gampell: "Therapeutic Abortion: A Problem in Law and Medicine," *Stanford Law Review*, Vol. 11 (1958–1959), pp. 417–455.

5. Smith, *Abortion and the Law*, pp. 37–59.
6. Selected from "Indications for Termination of Pregnancy," *British Medical Journal*, 1968, Vol. 1, p. 171.
7. R. F. Tredgold, "Psychiatric Indications for Termination of Pregnancy," *Lancet*, 1964, Vol. 2, pp. 1251–1254.
8. Sloane, "The Unwanted Pregnancy," Cf. Kerstin Höök, "Refused Abortion: A Follow-up Study of 294 Women Whose Applications Were Refused by National Board of Health in Sweden," *Acta Psychiatrica Scandinavica*, Vol. 39 (Supp. 168), (1963), pp. 1–156; Martin Ekblad, "Induced Abortion on Psychiatric Grounds: A Follow-up Study of 479 Women," *Acta Psychiatrica et Neurologica Scandinavica*, (Supp. 99), (1955), pp. 1–238; E. W. Anderson, "Psychiatric Indications for Termination of Pregnancy," *Journal of Psychosomatic Research*, Vol. 10 (1966), pp. 127–134; Bengt J. Lindberg, "Vad gör den abortsökande kvinnan, när psykiatern sagt nej?" *Svenska Läkartidningen*, Vol. 45 (1948), pp. 1382–1395; Karl G. Dahlgren, *On Suicide and Attempted Suicide: A Psychiatric and Statistical Investigation* (Lund, Sweden: Universitats Bokhander, 1945).
9. Myre Sim, "Abortion and the Psychiatrist," *British Medical Journal*, Vol. 2 (1963), pp. 145–148; correspondence, *ibid.*, pp. 1061–1062.
10. Sloane, "The Unwanted Pregnancy."
11. Z. Alexander Aarons, "Therapeutic Abortion and the Psychiatrist," *American Journal of Psychiatry*, Vol. 124 (1967), pp. 745–754.
12. Joseph Rheingold, in Cooke, *The Terrible Choice*, p. 78.
13. Sim, "Abortion and the Psychiatrist," p. 1455.
14. Abraham Heller and H. G. Whittington, "The Colorado Story: Denver General Hospital Experience with the Change in the Law on Therapeutic Abortions," *American Journal of Psychiatry*, Vol. 125 (1968), pp. 809–816.
15. *New York Times*, November 24, 1968.
16. *Medical World News*, May 23, 1963, p. 39.
17. U.S. Department of Labor, *Report on Family Law*, p. 29.
18. Smith, *Abortion and the Law*, p. 70. See also Roemer, "Abor-

tion Law," p. 1906, and Lars Huldt, "Outcome of Pregnancy When Legal Abortion is Readily Available," *Lancet*, 1968, Vol. 1, pp. 467–468.

19. Smith, *Abortion and the Law*, p. 28.

chapter seven • RECOMMENDATIONS

1. Erik H. Erikson, *The Young Man Luther* (New York: Norton, 1958), p. 70.
2. U.S. Department of Labor, *Report on Family Law*.
3. *Ibid.*, dissenting opinion, pp. 60–61.
4. "The Expectant Father Protected: Tort Action Allowed Against Abortionist," *Stanford Law Review*, Vol. 14 (1962), p. 901.
5. Cf. Sloane, "The Unwanted Pregnancy," and Huldt, "Outcome of Pregnancy."

INDEX

INDEX

GAP COMMITTEES, MEMBERS, AND OFFICERS
(*as of October 1, 1969*)

COMMITTEES

ADOLESCENCE
Joseph D. Noshpitz, Washington, D.C., *Chairman*
Warren J. Gadpaille, Denver, Colo.
Mary O'Neil Hawkins, New York, N.Y.
Charles A. Malone, Philadelphia, Pa.
Silvio J. Onesti, Jr., Boston, Mass.
Vivian Rakoff, Toronto, Canada
Calvin F. Settlage, San Francisco, Calif.
Sidney L. Werkman, Washington, D.C.

AGING
Jack Weinberg, Chicago, Ill., *Chairman*
Robert N. Butler, Washington, D.C.
Alvin I. Goldfarb, New York, N.Y.
Lawrence F. Greenleigh, Los Angeles, Calif.
Maurice E. Linden, Philadelphia, Pa.
Prescott W. Thompson, Topeka, Kans.
Montague Ullman, Brooklyn, N.Y.

CHILD PSYCHIATRY
E. James Anthony, St. Louis, Mo., *Chairman*
James M. Bell, Canaan, N.Y.
H. Donald Dunton, New York, N.Y.
Joseph M. Green, Madison, Wis.
John F. Kenward, Chicago, Ill.
William S. Langford, New York, N.Y.
John F. McDermott, Jr., Honolulu, Hawaii
Suzanne T. van Amerongen, Boston, Mass.
Exie E. Welsch, New York, N.Y.
Virginia N. Wilking, New York, N.Y.

THE COLLEGE STUDENT
Harrison P. Eddy, New York, N.Y., *Chairman*

69

Robert L. Arnstein, New Haven, Conn.
Alfred Flarsheim, Chicago, Ill.
Alan Frank, Albuquerque, N.Mex.
Malkah Tolpin Notman, Brookline, Mass.
Kent E. Robinson, Towson, Md.
Earle Silber, Washington, D.C.
Benson R. Snyder, Cambridge, Mass.
Tom G. Stauffer, Scarsdale, N.Y.

THE FAMILY
Norman L. Paul, Cambridge, Mass., *Chairman*
Israel Zwerling, New York, N.Y.
Ivan Boszormenyi-Nagy, Philadelphia, Pa.
L. Murray Bowen, Chevy Chase, Md.
David Mendell, Houston, Tex.
Joseph Satten, Topeka, Kans.
Kurt O. Schlesinger, San Francisco, Calif.
John P. Spiegel, Waltham, Mass.
Lyman C. Wynne, Bethesda, Md.

GOVERNMENTAL AGENCIES
Harold Rosen, Baltimore, Md., *Chairman*
Calvin S. Drayer, Philadelphia, Pa.
Edward O. Harper, Cleveland, Ohio
John E. Nardini, Washington, D.C.
Donald B. Peterson, Fulton, Mo.
Robert L. Williams, Gainesville, Fla.

INTERNATIONAL RELATIONS
Byrant M. Wedge, West Medford, Mass., *Chairman*
Francis F. Barnes, Chevy Chase, Md.
Eugene Brody, Baltimore, Md.
William D. Davidson, Washington, D.C.

Joseph T. English, Washington, D.C.
Louis C. English, Pomona, N.Y.
Frank Fremont-Smith, Massapequa, N.Y.
Robert L. Leopold, Philadelphia, Pa.
John A. P. Millet, New York, N.Y.
Alain J. Sanseigne, New York, N.Y.
Bertram Schaffner, New York, N.Y.
Mottram P. Torre, New Orleans, La.

MEDICAL EDUCATION
David R. Hawkins, Charlottesville, Va., *Chairman*
Hugh T. Carmichael, Washington, D.C.
Robert S. Daniels, Chicago, Ill.
Raymond Feldman, Boulder, Colo.
Saul I. Harrison, Ann Arbor, Mich.
Harold I. Lief, Philadelphia, Pa.
John E. Mack, Boston, Mass.
William L. Peltz, Philadelphia, Pa.
David S. Sanders, Los Angeles, Calif.
Robert A. Senescu, Albuquerque, N.Mex.
Roy M. Whitman, Cincinnati, Ohio

MENTAL HEALTH SERVICES
Lee G. Sewall, N. Little Rock, Ark., *Chairman*
Morris E. Chafetz, Boston, Mass.
Merrill Eaton, Omaha, Nebr.
James B. Funkhouser, Richmond, Va.
Robert S. Garber, Belle Mead, N.J.
Ernest W. Klatte, Talmage, Calif.
Alan I. Levenson, Tuscon, Ariz.
W. Walter Menninger, Topeka, Kans.

Lucy D. Ozarin, Bethesda, Md.
Jack A. Wolford, Pittsburgh, Pa.

MENTAL RETARDATION
Henry H. Work, Los Angeles, Calif., *Chairman*
Howard V. Bair, Parsons, Kans.
Peter W. Bowman, Pownal, Me.
Stuart M. Finch, Ann Arbor, Mich.
Leo Madow, Philadelphia, Pa.
Irving Philips, San Francisco, Calif.
George Tarjan, Los Angeles, Calif.
Warren T. Vaughan, Jr., San Mateo, Calif.
Thomas G. Webster, Chevy Chase, Md.

PREVENTIVE PSYCHIATRY
Stephen Fleck, New Haven, Conn., *Chairman*
Gerald Caplan, Boston, Mass.
Jules V. Coleman, New Haven, Conn.
Leonard J. Duhl, Berkeley, Calif.
Albert J. Glass, Oklahoma City, Okla.
Benjamin Jeffries, Harper Woods, Mich.
E. James Lieberman, Washington, D.C.
Mary E. Mercer, Nyack, N.Y.
Herbert C. Modlin, Topeka, Kans.
Harris B. Peck, Bronx, N.Y.
Marvin E. Perkins, New York, N.Y.
Harold M. Visotsky, Chicago, Ill.

PSYCHIATRY AND LAW
Zigmond M. Lebensohn, Washington, D.C., *Chairman* 1966–1969
Alan A. Stone, Cambridge, Mass., *Chairman* 1969–
Edward T. Auer, St. Louis, Mo.

John Donnelly, Hartford, Conn.
Jay Katz, New Haven, Conn.
Carl P. Malmquist, Minneapolis, Minn.
Seymour Pollack, Los Angeles, Calif.
Gene L. Usdin, New Orleans, La.
Andrew S. Watson, Ann Arbor, Mich.

PSYCHIATRY AND RELIGION
Earl A. Loomis, Jr., New York, N.Y., *Chairman*
Sidney S. Furst, New York, N.Y.
Stanley A. Leavy, New Haven, Conn.
Albert J. Lubin, Woodside, Calif.
Mortimer Ostow, New York, N.Y.
Bernard L. Pacella, New York, N.Y.

PSYCHIATRY AND SOCIAL WORK
John A. MacLeod, Cincinnati, Ohio, *Chairman*
C. Knight Aldrich, Chicago, Ill.
Maurice R. Friend, New York, N.Y.
John C. Nemiah, Boston, Mass.
Eleanor A. Steele, Denver, Colo.

PSYCHIATRY IN INDUSTRY
Harry H. Wagenheim, Philadelphia, Pa., *Chairman*
Spencer Bayles, Houston, Tex.
Thomas L. Brannick, Rochester, Minn.
Herbert L. Klemme, Topeka, Kans.
Jeptha R. MacFarlane, Westbury, N.Y.
Alan A. McLean, New York, N.Y.
Kenneth J. Munden, Memphis, Tenn.
Clarence J. Rowe, St. Paul, Minn.
Graham C. Taylor, Montreal, Canada

71

Psychopathology

Albert J. Silverman, New Brunswick, N.J., *Chairman*
Wagner H. Bridger, New York, N.Y.
Neil R. Burch, Houston, Tex.
Sanford I. Cohen, New Orleans, La.
Daniel X. Freedman, Chicago, Ill.
Milton Greenblatt, Boston, Mass.
Paul E. Huston, Iowa City, Iowa
P. Herbert Leiderman, Palo Alto, Calif.
Jack H. Mendelson, Chevy Chase, Md.
Richard E. Renneker, Los Angeles, Calif.
George E. Ruff, Philadelphia, Pa.
Charles Shagass, Philadelphia, Pa.
George E. Vaillant, Boston, Mass.

Public Education

Peter A. Martin, Detroit, Mich., *Chairman*
Leo H. Bartemeier, Baltimore, Md.
H. Waldo Bird, El Paso, Tex.
Lloyd C. Elam, Nashville, Tenn.
Dana L. Farnsworth, Cambridge, Mass.
James A. Knight, New Orleans, La.
John P. Lambert, Katonah, N.Y.
Mildred Mitchell-Bateman, Charleston, S.C.
Mabel Ross, Boston, Mass.
Julius Schreiber, Washington, D.C.
Miles F. Shore, Boston, Mass.
Kent A. Zimmerman, Berkeley, Calif.

Research

Morris A. Lipton, Chapel Hill, N.C., *Chairman*
Stanley Eldred, Belmont, Mass.
Louis A. Gottschalk, Irvine, Calif.
Sheppard G. Kellam, Chicago, Ill.

Donald F. Klein, Glen Oaks, N.Y.
Gerald L. Klerman, New Haven, Conn.
Ralph R. Notman, Brookline, Mass.
Alfred H. Stanton, Belmont, Mass.
Eberhard H. Uhlenhuth, Chicago, Ill.

Social Issues

Perry Ottenberg, Philadelphia, Pa., *Chairman*
Viola W. Bernard, New York, N.Y.
Lester Grinspoon, Boston, Mass.
Joel S. Handler, Chicago, Ill.
Judd Marmor, Los Angeles, Calif.
Roy W. Menninger, Topeka, Kans.
Arthur A. Miller, Chicago, Ill.
Peter B. Neubauer, New York, N.Y.
Charles A. Pinderhughes, Boston, Mass.
Kendon W. Smith, Piermont, N.Y.

Therapeutic Care

Bernard H. Hall, Topeka, Kans., *Chairman*
Ian L. W. Clancey, Ottawa, Canada
Thomas E. Curtis, Chapel Hill, N.C.
Robert W. Gibson, Towson, Md.
Harold A. Greenberg, Bethesda, Md.
Henry U. Grunebaum, Boston, Mass.
Lester H. Rudy, Chicago, Ill.
Melvin Sabshin, Chicago, Ill.
Benjamin Simon, Boston, Mass.
Robert E. Switzer, Topeka, Kans.

Therapy

Peter H. Knapp, Boston, Mass., *Chairman*

Henry W. Brosin, Pittsburgh, Pa.
Eugene Meyer, Baltimore, Md.
William C. Offenkrantz, Chicago, Ill.

Lewis L. Robbins, Glen Oaks, N.Y.
Albert E. Scheflen, Bronx, N.Y.
Harley C. Shands, New York, N.Y.
Lucia E. Tower, Chicago, Ill.

MEMBERS

Malcolm J. Farrell, Waverley, Mass.

CONTRIBUTING MEMBERS
Marvin L. Adland, Chevy Chase, Md.
Carlos C. Alden, Jr., Williamsville, N.Y.
William H. Anderson, Lansing, Mich.
Kenneth E. Appel, Ardmore, Pa.
M. Royden C. Astley, Pittsburgh, Pa.
Charlotte Babcock, Pittsburgh, Pa.
Grace Baker, New York, N.Y.
Bernard Bandler, Boston, Mass.
Walter E. Barton, Washington, D.C.
Anne R. Benjamin, Chicago, Ill.
Ivan C. Berlien, Coral Gables, Fla.
Sidney Berman, Washington, D.C.
Grete L. Bibring, Cambridge, Mass.
Edward G. Billings, Denver, Colo.
Carl A. L. Binger, Cambridge, Mass.
Wilfred Bloomberg, Hartford, Conn.
C. H. Hardin Branch, Salt Lake City, Utah
Matthew Brody, Brooklyn, N.Y.
Ewald W. Busse, Durham, N.H.
Dale C. Cameron, Geneva, Switzerland
Norman Cameron, New Haven, Conn.

Robert Coles, Cambridge, Mass.
Harvey H. Corman, New York, N.Y.
Frank J. Curran, New York, N.Y.
Bernard L. Diamond, Berkeley, Calif.
Franklin G. Ebaugh, Denver, Colo.
Joel Elkes, Baltimore, Md.
O. Spurgeon English, Narbeth, Pa.
Jack R. Ewalt, Boston, Md.
James H. Ewing, Wallingford, Pa.
Edward C. Frank, Louisville, Ky.
Lawrence Z. Freedman, Chicago, Ill.
Moses M. Frohlich, Ann Arbor, Mich.
Daniel H. Funkenstein, Boston, Mass.
Maurice H. Greenhill, Scarsdale, N.Y.
John H. Greist, Indianapolis, Ind.
Roy R. Grinker, Chicago, Ill.
Ernest M. Gruenberg, Poughkeepsie, N.Y.
Herbert I. Harris, Boston, Mass.
J. Cotter Hirschberg, Topeka, Kans.
Edward J. Hornick, New York, N.Y.
Roger William Howell, Ann Arbor, Mich.
Joseph Hughes, Philadelphia, Pa.
Portia Bell Hume, Berkeley, Calif.
Robert W. Hyde, Waterbury, Vt.
Lucie Jessner, Washington, D.C.
Irene M. Josselyn, Phoenix, Ariz.

73

Marion E. Kenworthy, New York, N.Y.
Othilda Krug, Cincinnati, Ohio
Lawrence S. Kubie, Sparks, Md.
Paul V. Lemkau, Baltimore, Md.
Maurice Levine, Cincinnati, Ohio
David M. Levy, New York, N.Y.
Robert J. Lifton, Woodbridge, Conn.
Erich Lindemann, Boston, Mass.
Reginald S. Lourie, Washington, D.C.
Alfred O. Ludwig, Boston, Mass.
Sydney G. Margolin, Denver, Colo.
Helen V. McLean, Chicago, Ill.
Karl Menninger, Topeka, Kans.
James G. Miller, Cleveland, Ohio
Angel N. Miranda, Hato Rey, Puerto Rico
Rudolph G. Novick, Lincolnwood, Ill.
Francis J. O'Neill, Central Islip, N.Y.
Humphry F. Osmond, Princeton, N.J.
Dane G. Prugh, Denver, Colo.
Franz K. Reichsman, Brooklyn, N.Y.
Eveoleen N. Rexford, Cambridge, Mass.
Milton Rosenbaum, New York, N.Y.
Mathew Ross, Chestnut Hill, Mass.

W. Donald Ross, Cincinnati, Ohio
Elvin V. Semrad, Boston, Mass.
Edward Stainbrook, Los Angeles, Calif.
Brandt F. Steele, Denver, Colo.
Rutherford B. Stevens, New York, N.Y.
Lloyd J. Thompson, Chapel Hill, N.C.
Harvey J. Tompkins, New York, N.Y.
Arthur F. Valenstein, Cambridge, Mass.
Helen Stochen Wagenheim, Philadelphia, Pa.
Raymond W. Waggoner, Ann Arbor, Mich.
Robert S. Wallerstein, San Francisco, Calif.
Edward M. Weinshel, San Francisco, Calif.
Joseph B. Wheelwright, San Francisco, Calif.
Cecil L. Wittson, Omaha, Nebr.
David Wright, Providence, R.I.
Stanley F. Yolles, Bethesda, Md.

LIFE MEMBERS
S. Spafford Ackerly, Louisville, Ky.
Hyman S. Lippman, St. Paul, Minn.
Francis H. Sleeper, Augusta, Maine

OFFICERS

President: John Donnelly
Vice President: George Tarjan
Secretary-Treasurer: Jack A. Wolford

Assistant Secretary-Treasurer: Jack Weinberg

PUBLICATIONS BOARD